C000229862

Quiver

For Michael

Quiver

Deryn Rees-Jones

seren

Seren is the book imprint of
Poetry Wales Press Ltd
Nolton Street, Bridgend, Wales, CF31 3BN
www.seren-books.com

ISBN 1-85411-354-2
A CIP record for this title is available from the British Library.

The publisher acknowledges the financial assistance
of the Welsh Books Council.

Printed in Perpetua by CPD (Wales), Ebbw Vale

For God mingles not with man; but through Love
all the intercourse and converse of god with man,
whether awake or asleep, is carried on.

Plato, *Symposium*, 'The Nature and Origin of Love'

I

The Cemetery

I've learnt to run, like an adult learns to sing,
the arpeggios of the body's muscles,
the biomechanics of the human scale,
forcing a life to be suddenly spoken,
a finger pressed to an ivory key, a note that issues
from an opened mouth, as if God or the gods
were already there, endorphins pulsing through
                                        the system,
the body's flux when contained in movement,
your hard-earned place in the world
on hold; I've learnt to take tarmac under my shoe,
to feel the spark between muscle and sinew
pushing the globe on its tilted axis,
the rib cage and its nesting heart,
ventricular walls and the pump of oxygen,
the flexion-extension of shoulder and arm
as you travel through light and a briskness of shadow,
suddenly animal, curious, terrible,
just for a moment never-grown-old....

It's the cemetery I run through now,
the snow-littered pathways of ordered mayhem,
the furnishings of its strange allotment,
recording angels, bears, dogs, gnomes,
a broken vase, a fading wreath, a votive candle
snow's snuffed out, Our Lady of Suburbia,

a rosary entwined in sculpted fingers,
propped beside a smiling Buddha, a paper blue
chrysanthemum wilting in his hand.

Yet, through the wreckage of doggerel,
on marble, on granite, through the hum of cars
on the circling road, through the cool swathes of air
on this mist-hung morning,
a blackbird opens its feathery throat
pulling the sky and the skyline closer
so hedgerow and barbed wire and railing,

the crunch of my footsteps on glistening paths,
rise up together, clash and unite,

when suddenly I stumble, hit the ground,
become myself stretched out among the graves,
the frost, a plot of orange dirt. Slumped beside me,
shouldered by a gravestone,
ice keeping death alive, a woman's ruined body,
pierced with an arrow like a fallen bird.
What is it like to know death so slowly,
hair and fingernails still growing
like Lizzie Siddall's in the grave?
What is it like – the presence of absence –
the space you keep in that clenched right hand?

It's a body I know from snapshots, old albums
carrying histories, other lives, other selves.

William and Mara. Mara and Will.
There at the mouth, carved like a seraph's,
a dash, a dart, an outpost of blood.
Her eyes are ash-pits in saintly expression
like Christ's on the cross in an incense-fuelled church,
or that woman of sorrows – the mother, the lover –?
a flash like lightning in her crow-dark hair.

I think of her now, the twist of flesh
on her stripped lean torso, remember a smile,
a forthright look. I pick myself up
and my stomach retches;
I dizzy, double over, then throw up.
The movie I'm in is in black and white.
I note an absence of birdsong, the moan of the thaw.
Then the soundtrack arrests.
Was I wrong, then, I wonder, remembering this,
how a voice from on high chastens us, comforts us.

Everything's still.

Underworld

Two policemen ferry me home.
I'm adrift in silence, a migraine of lights.
There's blood in my mouth, a taste of metal

like a coin placed under my tongue.

The Story of a Life

Will's home already, the dinner's on
as the house takes on his print.
I see him through the window,
gathering the light in shadows,
sitting with a cup, I guess,
of camomile and limeflower,
Bird playing as he reads his book.
Time swings back and forth
as evening is exposed.
Our ancestors collude in corners.
My grandparents from Bethesda, Liverpool.
His grandfather from Tipperary,
grandmother from Guangzhou.
I see them speaking Welsh/Chinese
and sipping Guinness in a brilliant pagoda.
Two dragons – east and west – collide.
And though I've phoned to say I'm late,
how will it be when he smiles, looks up
from the stories of Sui Sin Far,
when he says, "Listen to the story
of *My Chinese Husband*",
the month-old baby with his newly-shaved head;
or begins to tell me of his day at the hospital,
a woman with five foetuses inside her
they think they'll bring to term,
the woman he's been treating for three years

still waiting for a sperm, an egg;
how will it be when
I have to tell him,
when this narrative arrests
and the past opens
and time wobbles
and what I have to tell
becomes at once too long, too short?

Flashback

How does a photograph become a memory?
This one's not even mine. But I remember
Mara, grave as a kore, her sweater sleeves rolled.

How can I feel it, even now? The look on her face
as she guts a pair of rainbow trout;
in one swift action removes each head,

cleaving a knife that glints like quicksilver
dull against the papery bone.

Sky Canoe

I see, not feel, how beautiful they are.
                                    S.T.C.

Sometimes this bed without love, this
settling to sleep like children,
hand-in-hand, knees fitted into knees,
the radio on low, our books, clothes,
daily lives strewn carelessly about the floor

is both more and less than I can bear.
Take this sky the night has given us —
not the Pleiades or the Seven Sisters,
Cassiopeia with her train of hair —
but a heaven we have made ourselves,
the bright planets of our bedroom firmament

glow-in-the-dark plastic stars
fixed to a painted square.

Arrangements

We've no idea whether to bury her or send her to the flames.
Next of kin, Will settles on a pale oak box, and
like a wedding dress the length of it,
a sheath of snow-white flowers.

My Husband, Will

I've loved him for seven years, loved him
in a way that means I always want to look.

It's something in the eyes,
the way that beauty wanders slowly into you

even now, as he sits there in his shirtsleeves,
his shoulders slightly hunched

against the darkness, as he slips into his book.
So why do I see them as I do,

there in a pause as the past drapes round us,
his hand a compass, her spine a map,

or as children, now, playing hopscotch or tag,
as her dark eyes flash — are they touching tongues? —

and he drapes his arm about her neck.
When I look in the mirror it is her face

not mine. The weight of the coffin on Will's shoulder
hurts me like the weight of love.

The Funeral

I hardly know anybody here.
Some friends of Will I nod to:
a white-haired man,
a blonde in black whose beauty is too telling,
a group of Goths, their make-up running.

Someone in a creased grey suit
reads a passage from the Bible
which, of course, I recognise:

Ecclesiastes VII.iii

When Will sits slowly, heavily beside me,
his head is bowed. We're holding a space
like life between us. The congregation murmurs, kneels,
becomes a row of question marks interrogating darkness,
a shaft of sudden light.

Block

I'd taken leave on Will's advice;
taken a year to remember myself,
left the university, philosophers,
taken time for the body, and simpler thoughts.
What use is a poet who doesn't write?
And for a while, it helped,
those blue and yellow pills like magic beans:
nothingness trapped like a leaf in amber,
sunshine pouring out.

Tail

He's watched me for two days, this plainclothes policeman
with uncertain eyes, a paunch, a greying crop:

he's familiar, now, with that over-the-shoulder, don't-
hurt-me look, the way I throw it to the middle-distance,

unaware, on visits to the library, friends,
how space between us now is documented, marked.

He marvels at my knack of disappearing into doors,
how with a half-turn of the head

I can transform the everyday so swiftly,
silk handkerchiefs pulled from a folded palm,

a dove emerging from a hat. The outline of my frame,
now scattered in a mist of dust and light,

reminds him of the fingerprints he took, rolling each finger
across the page; fingers, he saw, still stained with ink

sitting beside me in the church to send the body off.
And my black Nissan

is quiet as a hearse, neither ghost nor echo,
the stretch of my shadow his only hope

as he follows me like a train of thought
through light-slicked, empty streets.

A Change in the Weather

Green shoots spike the frost
like secrets, promises that haunt us.
The sky is a mirror for space and light.
Yet something's not right.
Leaves fall in springtime like waterless koi,
unwanted gifts of exotic fruit.

Wonderland

Those wonder pills, their chemistry of light,
still keep me in a funny place,
as Erica, my oldest friend,
brings tea in willow-pattern cups,
her pregnant belly eight months heavy,
her hair a corona of auburn curls.

I feel like Alice in her flooded house.

At every corner now, or so it seems, is Mara's face,
a Cheshire Cat which grins and disappears.

And no one has the words I need,
till Erica, with a look I read
as either faith or doubt, her baby daughter
uncannily like her, curled up on her knees,
sends me home with a kiss, an unreadable smile:

"Pick up your pen and write."

Ghosts

The dead are with us still
however we love or lose them.
Where do they live, the ghosts we try to kill?
The dead are with us. Still
they wear us as they will,
sing us like a nursery rhyme, a hymn,
make something inside us irretrievably small
however we love or lose them.

Ash Wednesday

I'm in the Bluebird driving home
as morning finds itself in clear white skies,

the mass at St Nick's at the Pier Head failing me, finding
no place in me for words of faith,

just a sharp space in my upturned heart that might
be anywhere: a small white cup, a shattered vase,

when there, at the lights I swear I see her:
her straight body, those even shoulders,

combat trousers, a ballerina cardigan in grey,
her hair wound up in a silver dragon clip,

gold flashes, like wings, on brilliant white Nike.
As the lights change I count to ten,

turn the nearest corner, look again.
Of course, she's disappeared,

then I glimpse the dog
tethered to a railing near the top end

of the street. "Wait!" and I call her name.
But as soon as she's there, she's gone,

part *bandolero*, part *bas bleu*.
And all I have left is my dumb reflection,

the blurt of horns, the misted windscreen,
ash on my forehead, tears on my cheeks.

Liverpool Blues

The skyline in the moonlight, the river running thin,
my lover weeping lotus blossom for his next of kin.
The stars will tell their stories over Birkenhead and Camell Laird's.

In Berry Street, in Bold Street, in Princes Park and Princess Street
I've seen a girl I never knew and never thought to meet.
The Liver Birds have flown away, the cathedrals' doors are closed.

In hospitals and factories, bars, clubs, churches, loony bins,
something is uneasy beneath the city's restless din.
A woman has been murdered, yet no one says a word.

The homeless and the helpless, the workers on the street
have nothing left to live for, can only smell defeat.
My husband's left his heart elsewhere, my love has been foreclosed.

We're living in a borderland, somewhere between life and death,
losing ourselves in the search for a self.
It's a country of our making, the cards are curiously dealt.

The helicopter spotlights buzz us, lights come flooding in,
even our bedroom's no longer safe, we're living on a pin.
We mouth our dreams in the telling dark, but nothing can be heard.

We mouth our dreams in the telling dark, but nothing can be heard.

We mouth our dreams in the telling dark, and only words are lost.

We mouth our dreams in the telling dark, still nothing can be heard.

Good Cop, Bad Cop

They must practise their clichés till they know them by heart,
say their lines with this look as they play their part.
One drinks coffee with a dash of cold water.
And the one I've met before,
his firm hand cool at my greeting,
refuses to drink anything at all.

TIME OF DEATH.
CAUSE OF DEATH.
Found with the body, this:
a bundle of hand-written papers – poems? –
a bunch of unmarked keys.

Bad cop slaps them on the table.

I'm meant to answer questions.

Good cop swills the dregs of coffee cooling, refuses to
                                                    look up.

I recognise the keys as Will's, the writing as my own:

Quiver

Let's start with the stag.
No hedging, no prevarication,
no semiotics or white lies.
Let's start, simply, with this tale of transformation.
Artemis and Actaeon. As good as any other.
I'll begin by simply asking you,
Imagine this! The weight of the antlers,
the stagginess of the moulting coat;
the staggy eyes with their bushy lashes,
the intimacy of the moment
when for the first time
a man sees the body of a woman.
And then this man becomes a stag.
Let's start with the Dewars poster on the wall,
his proud glance,
let's start with the head at the feet of the huntsman,
the stag's blood, his rite of passage
daubed on his skin as if accidents with a razor
— the cheek-torn, cotton-woolly kind —
were all it took to make a man of him;
Let's start with what he once was
that day as he peeked and pried,
a young man, bold as brass,
in those days when seeing was doing,
the eucalyptus whispering
as this woman undresses

who is also a god. And while he watches her,
as water somehow possesses her,
rids the privacy of her well-formed body,
then gives itself up
like the body gives up perfume, sweat,
revealing her, as she emerges
clavicle, breast-bone,
the blue vein at her child-free nipple,
the thatch of hair that covers the pubis:
Artemis, single-minded,
casting about red-cheeked,
groping for her bow and arrow
refusing to be naked for this man.
That's when the story starts,
with the divine inviolate,
that's where the story starts
in the terrible comedy of shame.
And when we ask how desire runs —
upwards on the spine's ladder, to the nape,
and down again
on that central point
between labia and coccyx,
that private space the huntsman longed for,
perhaps wanted to bring
between thumb and forefingers
to know in himself interior joy —
we must ask then why desire that runs
between humans and gods
is always ill-fated as our story now

hangs on a breath, as we pin back our ears,
cut the umbilicus, its glistening thread...
Take Semele, consumed by fire
in the face of Zeus, Dionysis her son
left to mature in the incubator of
his father's thigh, a scrawny cry
as he was born, wriggling
from his tight papoose; or that bright nymph
Echo, known for her poetry, heartbreaking songs,
damned by Hera till her bones turned to stone
and her voice a whisper; Narcissus her lover,
condemned to keep looking,
transformed to a lonesome waterside flower....
But let's shift back our focus
to Actaeon / Artemis, and the goddess's companion
who had also spotted our peeping Tom,
who longed to push her breasts against his back,
rub peplon and chiton against that chest
for whom chastity is a spiritual heist,
who covets most the watermark streaks,
stretchmarks on a mother's skin,
who in Titian's painting failed again
under the skull of a stag. Faith,
let's call her that, who wanted nothing more
than the spillage of silver,
who as she watched him watching them
as they undressed, slipped off her dress,
this time without caution,
holding her arms above her head,

prolonging the moment of her nudity,
airing the flex and tautness of her limbs
the narrow triangle of her unmarked back,
the downy base of that fragile neck.
Let's imagine what would have happened
had Artemis not spotted him.
For here it was, dark as a plum,
the genesis of a ruined moment,
the intoxication of a bird's first flight,
the rumination of the world,
a man aspiring to see the goddess,
And wanting what? To feel her goodness
not a violation; and a woman,
not a goddess, but infused with her goodness,
wanting to find a part of herself, in this man
as she felt his body as a line of pleasure:
it is done, here it is, we have done it, it is done.
For what she wanted was belief in a self.
What she wanted was to look at the goddess
to see something there of herself, too;
what she wanted
was to look at the man without fear or shame
with an image of herself with which to begin.
But that bronzed creature, which is where,
in a fashion, we began,
was no answer, as she peered into the bathing pool,
seeing the stag by her own face,
pregnant now, though she doesn't know it,
and the stag ripped apart by the hounds....

Those hounds! Imagined now as what?
An ever-changing line of mothers, daughters, long-lived women?
Antigone and Clytemnestra, Penelope and Joan.
The names might go on, being all things and nothing,
finding within themselves routes to becoming:
lovers of women, lovers of men. Names
trip off the tongue: Millicent, Sylvia,
Christabel, Emily, Angel Virginia, No-nonsense Simone,
Glorious Gloria, Unblushing Germaine;
Fierce Luce, Brave Julia, la belle Hélène.
They burn like a catechism, are worthy of praise.
Here's hound Catherine, now, with her crown of thorns,
Little Saint Bride with her cow-print jacket,
Agnes the Borzoi, the Windhound Poor Clare.
Here's Sappho, Felicia, Aphra, Christina,
so many Elizabeths they can't all be named.
But let us return now to Faith,
the mother perhaps of all invention,
tears pouring from her virgin cheeks,
still hoping to find herself, anywhere, anyhow,
witness to the spillage of blood,
as Actaeon, whom she has loved,
or the idea of him, who has made her unchaste,
is disembowelled, whose brave head, as she sees it,
lies ludicrous on the sandy floor.
She would light up the forest with candles, if she could,
wear his head like a headdress of candles,
so that wax and blood was intermingled,
would drip to her shoulders in rosy tears.

And yet, with her cold stare, now,
Artemis at her shaking side,
patron of childbirth and chastity,
the double-voiced nature of her own creation,
with a miraculous stirring divorced from her body
scratches out words with a stick on the floor.
And the empty-eyed sky looks down, regardless,
as Faith dresses, rolls back her sleeves,
her eyes more knowing than she is telling
as she holds up a mirror to the goddess,
looks at herself, behind her, through it,
and on.

II

Quiet City

after Aaron Copland

So here I am in the dark wood,
not seeing life or love, for the trees,
wishing language could make of us something good,

the silence between us like the parted sea
as stern, in the blue light of the dash,
Will drives, refusing to look at me.

Then, out of the night, giving shape to our passage,
a line of music spills out on *3*,
a trumpet of velvet rising from ash

as we slip with a gear change, a glance, through the quiet city,
unstrung, unlovely, but awake to movement's curve and bend
as I roll down windows, let air meet the body.

The city's left me spellbound,
opened me to a quiet magic: the ferrying river's riffling intent.
So we balance in the moment, lost from language, without god

or gods as music speaks at the silent heart of us. It's a
                                        sudden shift
as rift becomes raft, live, love.
I'm learning not to measure myself against it, this wish for
                                        the spirit

to burn open my mouth, to break me open or somehow move
me, for the night like a gift of myrrh, instead to spill
its ordinary perfume, as rain begins to fall on distant roofs.

Symposium: The Geneticist's Dinner

Tonight the talk's of twins and clones
a parlour game of metaphors to illustrate
the double helix of DNA.

Will has some things to say.
And because I've published a book,
a staccato treatise on cloning ethics

and our perception of death
– last year, a lifetime ago –
I'm expected to respond.

I try hard to remember a line of thought,
reel in the Virgin Mary,
Athena sprung from the head of Zeus,

the Groundhog day of our human frailties,
anticipated but unfelt,
the fake promise of perpetual life,

but my sentences, like some decomposition,
lie like a corpse, are eaten away.
Before we leave, Nate Devine, confident,

a white-haired man with a tongue of glass
I remember from the funeral
asks if I'll give his faculty a talk next month.

Carefully, I look at him.
He's like some well-dressed dazzly god.
I take his card and say I'll call.

He bothers me with his eyes and laughs,
touches my arm like he's known me forever.
My cheeks redden for a moment

and then Will is there, and because I wanted it
we're walking home. The conversation's lifted us up
and for the first time in what seems a long time,

there's an alignment of the body and the mind.
Later we interrupt the night, the stars,
the kiss and bend and heat of us.

And because everything, these days,
comes down to death, I remember
the canopy of stars, the four poster

both coffin and confessional where he told me
of the burial he'd have, hostage to nothing
but air and light – a slow dismemberment

on the roof of the world, the smell of cedarwood and pine,
cleaned flesh and bones hurled up to the vultures –
those holy birds I'd learned to love.

Beatitude

I sing in praise of single things —
of spirogyra, starfish, hydra and amoeba,
chlamydomonas, protozoa, of plankton, aphids,
dandelions and waterfleas,
their simple replication.
I sing in praise of sea squirts, strawberries,
the whisperings of the aspen tree;
sing, too, the earthworm, its hermaphrodite wriggle,
the complicated gender games of clownfish,
the honeyed urgency of the unfrail bee.
And praise too, the heroic rabbit,
her cheerful lesson of reproduction,
those charts we drew in blue and red
in third form biology. Praise also
sperm and ovum's heady clash,
the headstrong ram that tups the ewe.
Let me equally praise the love between men,
the love between women; praise the foetus' kicks
on a colander heaven,
the sperm blown fresh in the mouth
of the lover, humming with life, electricity.
Praise rub and touch, ungainly hump,
the cool pipette, its righteous offspring;
praise, too, responsibility. Praise our desires.
Praise our desires to know and not know.
Praise all our progeny, the empty womb, the full.
Praise the will to become, love's credo.

A Second Sighting

I'm walking from Paradise Street where I left the car
when something changes: a droopy cloud wanders
across an uninked sky. Mothers with their kids in
buggies, stroll. Hawkers hawk, shoppers shop.
A seagull catches me with its yellow eye.
Sunshine dizzies me with its sudden wink.
Then everything says Mara. *How do I know?*
Even like this, the long coat, the hat pulled low.
I take her arm, and as she turns
my heart does cartwheels down a thousand steps,
slalom on a wintry piste.

Then

She takes my arm, says "Sssshhhh,"
pushes a note in my gaping pocket.
Her dark eyes are cool as a church,
fixing on mine, both query and quest.

Who's written this strange yet familiar script?
Who's following who?
Then she's off, and I'm left with her whisper,
a mark on my arm where her grip was too tight,
handwritten lines on an unlined page.

Night Drive II

What I love at night is that sense of departure,
the recklessness of an enormous soul
and all the threads of life undone.
I might be going anywhere
as the radio speaks in tongues, untuned.
The Bluebird clears its throat,
and borrowing Will's mobile,
I leave a scanty message and my number
with Erica as I drive, digits punched
like stars in the galaxy,
my new address a welcome prison tag.
Those little helpers, sunshine pills,
I've left in a drawer in a former life.
Maybe silence is the voice of God,
the breeze that floods the empty bedroom,
the scrawl of the unmade bed.

A Visitation

Here, in a patch of darkness in the Bluebird where I sit,
Liverpool opens like a rent in time. The centuries elide

to a collage of water, newspaper print.
The songs of the slaves with their branded foreheads

rise to the heavens in a shift of pain,
and then the refugees take up their song,

abandoned in an unknown port.
Choleric children shake and cry.

The angel of history throws back her shoulders,
her violet eyes look forwards and back.

And for the first time in a long time I feel that I could weep
as daytime's colours slip

inside each other, disappear.
I press the buzzer as instructed,

and the slow world turns.
I give a last look back at the roughed up night,

hold its memories close:
a street lamp, a dog bark,

orange, unearthly, bleak.

Limbo

For a while there's no movement, and no answer.
This rattling's the stenographer alive and remembering,
moving on silence and Canto V,
words bashed like braille into my head.
Then the door clicks a funny double click
and I'm in. Was it always this quiet,
with only the flickering heart
for company, walking fearfully into the dark
to meet the living dead?

Talking about the Weather

Was never on the cards, but she looks at me
with a look that blames the world.
"It's so cold in here", she says, shaking,
despite the weight of hair, her oddly androgynous
beautiful head.

Against Empiricism

I'm not sure exactly what I want,
searching for signs of life.
I feel like Saint Thomas slipping his hand
into the wounded side of God.

Chez Nous

She floods the world with light
and my eyes dilate to successive rooms
of highly-polished tables, chairs,
a room of baby Grands....
She's sleeping in a storeroom;
stacked-up haphazardly on shelves
old pots, cracked jars; there's a
rising smell of creosote and polish,
the whiff of joiner's glue.
From a peeling plaster wall
a stag's head looms.
His glass eyes glint. Beneath him, half-asleep,
the hound. From beneath lop-ears
a pair of doggy eyes look up.

Her words the only sound:
"The less I say the better" and her small pale mouth is set.
In a strange domestic moment
she offers me a cup of tea, hands me scissors
and a tarnished mirror, bends her head
to light a cigarette. Her face is clouded
for a moment in the smoke. There's little enough
to show she's here: a rucksack with a change
of clothes, dog-food in tins, a toothbrush,
a notebook, a dulled Swiss Army knife.
At a table, in the corner,

are papers bundled, tied with string,
and a fountain pen, sharp as an arrow,
dribbles ink onto a blotter,
a wreath of flowers
etched in its glinting nib.

The match smears the silence, a falling star.

"You'll just have to trust me. I need your help."

The Haircut

Am I saving her life with stories, or is she saving mine?

I take the hair in a trembling hand, slice it to the nape,
then start to layer it, bring it closer to the scalp.

It smells of borage and camphor oil,
falls to the floor like a twist of apple peel,

spelling out words with a life of their own.

Second Look

She's taller and broader than I'd thought:
like Artemis the hunter god,

chaste and secure in her life without men.

The Answerphone

I'm fiddling with the mobile's keypad,
when out of nowhere Erica's voice rings clear:

"Call me," a sigh, and then
a voice

I almost recognise:
"News on Mara."

The voice of glass makes its arrangements.

We are all gone into a world of light.

Promises to Keep

Midnight, and things are slowly sinking in.
My head light as an astronaut's
when behind me, out of the nowhere darkness
there's the rev of an engine, a shout of lights,
and before I know it
a balaclava'd face looms large,
its hands at the wheel of a low black car.
I throw myself back on the warehouse wall
as night reduces to a stab of pain.
I feel the Bluebird spin as it carries a blow,
note how a fractured line of pink graffiti
spells INNOCENT on the sooted brick,
then look to a sky empty of planets
as slowly I reach in my pocket for the keys.
I'm going to shout up to Mara then change my mind.
I crunch two painkillers from the glove-locker's hoard,
take a swig of flat Coke. My hand trembles
as I start the ignition, shift through the gears
as we limp towards home. I'm alive, amazed,
nursing my pride, my car's broken wing.

Doubting Will

And how do we come home,
I ask myself, moving beneath the lintel
bringing the outside in,
dropping car keys on the mantelpiece
abandoning my jacket to a chair,
Will's phone returned to his empty pocket
where even now it shakes me with its stare.
Somewhere a tap drips, riddles away
its slight sad song. I pull a beer from the fridge
and the kitchen brightens as I lean against
the counter top, run my hands through my hair.
My lips are cool as a ghost's on glass.
How do we find each other again, I wonder,
carefully locking doors and windows, flicking a switch
so the stairway softens with a lamp's pale glow.
I watch my hand on my chest as it falls and rises,
as my lungs blossom, as I slowly exhale.

Faith

Will's fast asleep, buried in pillows,
cocooned in the pastels of our wedding quilt.
I watch how his body moves,
the moments of being that make him, still.
I think how his life is breath as I pull his body
closer to mine. What dream is this?
What science that pulls the body's airs and gases
unaware? What electricity
that brings us in a moment here?
The look on his face like a sleeping soldier
in Piero's *Risen Christ*.

A Bout de Souffle

Breathless as the pill-dreams leave you
I'm left with what might be real or not:
Mara, shrunk to a tiny automaton,
balancing on my trembling eyelids,
slipping down my shoulders, leaping to the floor.
She shins up my knees like reticulate sorrow.
Her palms are bleeding.
There's an arrow in her heart.

Amour! Amour! she laughs,
her face a stone that's fallen from the heavens.

Her wings thrash a hailstorm, blow the night away.

Belief

There are things I want to believe.

In the absence of prayer I think about love.

White Nights

I'm a leper that sleep avoids:
my cropped head festering in the pillow
pupils narrowed by the tilted anglepoise.
In all the detective novels I've ever read,
like Oedipus, the protagonist
just has to know.
Is every tragedy so closed?

Quizmaster: Starter for ten.
How many Chandler novels can you name?

Contestant: *The Little Sister*, *Lady in the Lake*,
The Long Goodbye.

Quizmaster: Poor show.

A Dream

Last night I saw the future's ghost,
Its face was dimpled, eager.
It smiled and sucked but could not rest,
I asked it to draw near.

As white as snow, as black as jet,
It hovered in the air,
Plucked at my lips, my hands, my heart,
Warming the stratosphere.

As red as blood, as fresh as bile,
Its tongue about my ear,
It whispered that it now was time
To undo pain and fear.

It shimmered, glittered, floating near,
I felt its pulsing heart,
Yet when I touched its open lips
It quickly disappeared.

My hand was marked with wonder,
A stain bled from a flower,
My fingers like bright stamens,
My palm the pollen bower.

Perhaps it was a vision
That slipped before my eyes
And moved between this world of mine,
And what is not categorised.

Or else it was a trembling thought
Escaping from the brain,
The mouth amazed to open
To a voice that's not my own.

I had not sought to harm it
With arrow, shot or knife,
Unlike the albatross it lived
And living it was life.

Some said it was some female god
Descending from above,
Making a genealogy of souls
From her idea of love.

Others a life in utero,
Gametes hurled into the several world
Where male and female slipped away
And couldn't be recalled.

Sprung from a head in brilliance
Like a — collision — in the sky,
It was a melody of differences,
A snowflake drifting by.

It looked behind, it looked beyond,
It brought an eerie calm
As if the world was in my hands
And soothed a raging storm.

And through the hawthorn blossom
As my tears disturbed the night
I saw it wander through the sky
Radiating light.

Its edges smeared with brilliant dust
It scorched its silent way,
A chemistry of splitting cells
A bright infinity....

Decisions

And then my waking up, a slow arrival
at a face, the brushed and suited blue
of morning, a damp kiss pushed

on my still-parted lips. *Sweetheart.* A quick departure's
caught through half-closed eyes:
a shoulder and a trouser leg,

a ghostly polished shoe....
My dreams are spilling still,
fall from my eyes like pennies, creatures,

now, condemned to crawl in dust and corners,
dropping from my mouth.
The last squats on my chest and croaks, a

bright fire-bellied toad,
the heat and weight of which becomes enough
to burn the cool white sheets, take down the house,

erase the road, as flames run up
the street-lamps/blazing torches,
duplicate their orange glow

this sudden heat and untold fury,
bringing me round, with a gasp, at last,
settling in a line of sweat across my brow.

Following Will

I watch as he strolls across the university car park,
swipes his ID through the hesitant lock. Minutes later,

a small black Audi – behind the tinted glass
the driver like an arctic fox – silently draws up.

The porter, who knows me, nods me through.
I watch him through the glass partition as something

startles him, and he stoops to recover his fallen keys –
St Peter groping in the dark,

eternity, or the way into heaven, spilled from its fob like
$\qquad\qquad\qquad\qquad\qquad$ sycamore seeds –

A Confrontation

Still-life, freeze-frame. An office, innocent as a pot-plant:
Nate's room. Blue letters on his door.

Will has his head in his hands, a stack of photographs
beside him. I watch through dirty glass.

Here's Mara caught on camera, pale and thin,
back-dropped by concrete buildings daubed in
                                        Chinese characters.

Is this Shanghai, Beijing? Beside her half-clothed children
are playing in the scrubby grass. My thoughts race on.

From this doorway in the empty building
the strip-light threatens in its blinking repose

and Rach II plays to our brief encounter.
Nate gives his ghostly, unchanging smile

as I enter the scene, wondering even as he says it
if this is some terrible double bluff

dividing first from last, the sheep from the goats:
the woman who died, the woman I found

not a ghost I'd refused to believe in, but met,
not Lazarus, or some fierce angel,

not Mara, but her twin?

Clone
After PM

As *The Comedy of Errors* becomes *Twelfth Night*
and *A Stolen Life* becomes *The Double Life of Veronique*
and Aechmi becomes Amphitryon
and *Invasion of the Body Snatchers* becomes *The Stepford Wives*
and Mike Yarwood becomes Rory Bremner
and Marilyn Monroe becomes Madonna Ciccone
and Megan becomes Morag
and Dolly Parton becomes Dolly the Sheep
so this becomes you

As a Partridge in a Pear Tree becomes the One True God
and Eight Maids a Milking become the Eight Beatitudes
and Eleven Benevolent Elephants become Lovely Lemon
                                            Liniment
and No Motor Response becomes Obeys Commands
and "Do Geese see God" becomes "Dogma: I am God"
and the collected poems of Li Po becomes the *Celestial*
                              Empire of Benevolent Knowledge
and Confucius becomes confusion
and Moy becomes moi
so this becomes you

As the Neolithic becomes the Paleolithic
and *Alice in Wonderland* becomes *Alice Through the Looking Glass*
and *David Copperfield* becomes David Copperfield
and *Opportunity Knocks* becomes *Stars in Their Eyes*

and The Byrds become A Flock of Seagulls
and Melanie Klein becomes Calvin Klein
and the angel in the house becomes the angel of history
and George Bush becomes George W Bush
so this becomes you

As Mandelstam becomes Mandelson
and concomitant becomes commitment
and the King of Siam becomes Kojak
and the pea-flower becomes the black-bellied honey lover
and the madness of George III becomes Queen Victoria
and identical twins become mother and daughter
and affect becomes effect
and cwifer becomes quiver
so this becomes you

As Finisterre becomes Fitzroy
and Skin and Blister becomes Bricks and Mortar
and the good twin becomes the bad twin
and *Schmalz* becomes *Schadenfreude*
and Artemis becomes Diana
and *The Day of the Triffids* becomes *Gardeners' World*
and a shot in the dark becomes a shot in the arm
and vagina becomes penis, flowering in the shadowy womb
so this becomes you....

Liminal

I hover in between the spaces —
accident, coincidence, and truth —

Nate's expression benevolent, shrewd,
locked like a magnet into mine.

And Will upset, his features rearranging.
I imagine him the father of my child.

And all the time, like a pulse, a voice in my head
says something doesn't ring true. Why?

Because of something I read in Nate's cold eyes.
Mara, gone to the bad? Mara, like a phantom, gone.

III

"Above Us Only Sky"

Everything's still. An orchard of turf and stone, as I run.
Does thinking show me how to feel
or feeling help me how to think.
What is to be done?

I pass a gravedigger,
a woman in a headscarf with a face of tears,
standing by a common plot.
Is love the only game we play
with light and salt and air?
Is it only the pull of the earth
that learns to hold us down,
the spaces between grass and sky
we've always known are there?

The crime scene's yellow tape
reminds me. The white tape
of her absent body. What is this strange
return, a dangerous compulsion to repeat?
To slow-mo, rewind,
have the woman who's not Mara
hoisted by some unlawful force
turn to the camera in surprise
as the arrow flies backwards,
launches out of her. What do I want?
For words and worlds
to unwrite themselves?

Years split beneath the soil,
glitter like dew-fall in the shivery grass,

paper and circumstance suddenly blank.

A Vacillation

Erica's on the sofa with her feet up when I finally arrive.
She gives me that look I'm getting used to,
directs me to the bathroom where I do the test.

There, twinned on a strip of white plastic
like a miracle I walk across,
a drunk on trial,
arms stretched out, without a wobble,

life,
a thin blue line.

Warehouse Fugue

We say we want to buy a piano
which I sit and play

haltingly at first, and then
forgetting myself,

the weight of my forearm pushed into the keys
so notes resound throughout the warehouse.

I play to the bar-line in my head, and then repeat,
Go back to sign.

Erica, hovering, *faux distrait*,
makes like she's looking for the loo.

"We'd a classy gent from the hospital in here."
She makes polite enquiries.

But even then I know.

Square One

I rest my head on the Bluebird's wheel,
as Erica, rooting in her copious bag,

hands me a softbound notebook and that fountain pen.
"Found this," she grins

with a look that says
I believe you, at last.

It's what? A diary?
Times, places, dates,

fragments of poems
Mara's copied out.

One in particular snags at my heart:

Living had failed and death had failed,
And I was indeed alone.

And there as I look,
the date I found the body —

Feb. 11th — eerily blank.
Underlined, the 17th, tomorrow.

In Chinatown the New Year celebrations:
the lion who does the

lettuce-eating dance, the
dragon dance that binds the people

bringing luck and happiness into the streets.
Already Will has filled the house

with plum blossom, narcissus,
a bowl of kumquats in the hall.

That's where I want to be,
trusting, alive, lost

in an odour of fruit and flowers,
and a sudden life inside me

I'd like the chance to tell.

Good Cop Pays a Visit

And I wonder why he does this,
sugaring his coffee generously,
handing me a sheaf of papers.
"Let's think of them as a large red herring".
It seems I'm off the hook for now.
He's asking lots of questions, still.
How long has your husband known Nate Devine?
And Mara, how well did she know Nate?
Were they friends or colleagues, would you say?
What would you say to the layman
was the nature of the work?
Dr. Dupin brought us a letter, has serious concerns.
"I've reason to believe your life,
your husband's, are in danger."
(Does he speak to a script?)
I'm losing the plot, haven't time or space
to think how I want my story to go.

A Call

The phone call comes, as I thought it might:
Nate, elegant, easy, always shameless.
And I play along.

The patter, the silences, carefully executed,
beautifully planned.

We agree to meet,
"It's a bore", Nate drawls, "But bring that husband of yours.
This time at least. He tells me you've something I'd like to see."
He laughs.
Mid-day in Chinatown,
The Ming Kee, a tiny restaurant we've eaten at before.
"Much more of an authentic experience, wouldn't you say?"
And then, "Wear that dress," he commands.
"Like hell", I think, but wait in the pause,
then slowly put the receiver down.

Year of the Horse

We're both bulked up in bullet-proof vests,
Good Cop and Bad Cop materialised
into something more than CID.
Outside a stall sells paper windmills,
pendants for double-happiness,
fortune cookies, rings of jade.
I lose myself for a moment to the crowd:
an art student whose dreadlocks reach his knees,
two Chinese girls in silk, tiger-dragon,
cherry blossom, ribbons knotted in their hair.
A grey-faced man marks bets, props himself
against a wall; two boys in shirts,
one blue, one red, scuffle with a ball.
Peace through the four seasons!
Strong body and health!
May your wishes come true!
The parades, the crowds, the noise, the dances
have begun. And then
like something walking out of myth,
pulled from a vase in the British Museum,
in an elegant movement from start to finish
a familiar figure reaches for an arrow, loads a bow.
As Nate looks up, he's realised too late. *Mara!*
Seconds after there's a marksman's shot.
A splattering of firecrackers
echo in the street.
Year of the Horse.
And blood is all we know.

Take Two

For the second time I'm left with a corpse,
Nate with his arms stretched out,
his face laid down. A woman's voice
shouts in Chinese. And, like a miracle,
the archer's disappeared.
A man in black wearing a baseball cap
swears, "Glanced her!"
pushes across the stunned and weeping tables,
follows her out back.

I look to Will, but he's gone too.

I sit there, speechless.

On my upturned hands, on my throat,
blood mapping all the untidy routes of life,
the veins and arteries
that lie beneath the skin
like trembling tattoos.

An Ending

How far can a dying woman run
amid the sound of firecrackers and ambulances,
helicopters, sirens, the sudden brilliance of sky,
a small encroaching sun?
How far can Will, her best friend, follow,
and that dog, and those men, hot on their trail,
hounding a dying animal?
I'll let her go this far – past the Millennium arch
imported from Shanghai, failing now
as she skirts the Blackie, flying like the goddess
or the muse she is. Some poetic law of justice says
I'll leave her here: her breath coming fast but faint
on Hope Street, as I set her down
on the steps of a cathedral. *Let her die*
there in the arms of a man who can't save her,
stemming the bleeding with his hands, his shirt.
Leave them be, framed by stone, looking up at the sky,
and a figure of Christ looking out at the city,
his arms embracing the theatres and restaurants,
the students and prostitutes, the crown-like peaks
of another cathedral, the seagulls, the river,
the skyline, what is beyond.
And this man with a woman in his arms.
Let's stop up our ears to those
last words between them.
Let time give them their moment,
whoever they are.

A Change in the Weather

Green shoots spike the frost
like secrets, promises that haunt us.
Bulbs push through the earth.
The umbrella silks of their brilliant colours
are their own grave: for all flowers
are flowers of the dead.

The Lantern Festival

We've filled the house with candles.
Time enough for roaming the streets,
tonight is our own. The threads of the story
are unravelling. And even now, Will says,
he isn't sure, which one of them was Mara.
Sisters who for thirty years hadn't
known each other, finding each other
a birth and a death of the self, somehow.
But tonight the house is dancing to our light.
Grief sits, quelled for a while,
half-asleep, beside the snoozing hound.
Erica's here, with her day-old baby,
born in a pool as I crouched beside her
watching the face of her new son rise,
his tiny fingers dancing in water,
as he stares at us with some sweet surprise.
Blessings, little one as you softly feed. And little girl,
sucking your thumb beside your brother, curl up,
be at peace. Sleep for a while on these fire-side chairs.
Shadows flicker. And time begins.
Will throws another log across the fire.
A life flutters and turns inside me.
Elsewhere I've started to imagine.
Words spill across an empty page.

Relics

For Will

Different in shadows now, we look on at the evening,
the river like the name of someone unremembered,
a freckled arm, uncovered, a hemisphere of constellations
trailed across the sky. And so the soft straightforward night
begins with snowfall, snowdrifts – or do we just imagine that?–
as winter's ending colours us, imagines us as people
we have never been. And though a thousand different stories
quiver in the moment – a hand unclasped, a darting word
                                                        unsaid –
I don't look back. Familiar in a dream
somewhere, my cheek pressed to your shoulder,
our lives grow up between us. Like the glistening bones
of martyrs, saints, you hold about your person,
I remind you, as we drive "This is our tale",
and words our only keepsakes of the Bluebird's journey home.

Afterthought

for my daughter

I am following with my finger the blue veins
that travel from wrist to stoop of palm
as you lie now, little milk-drunk carcass,
in an accident of sleep. This is what mothers do

or what I've learned to do, to search your body
for signs of life, wary of pulse and breath
as all the time you follow me,
your mouth, insistent, through the night.

See! I have pressed the soft vowels of your imagination
and made them part of me. They pull me open, stitch me up,
your animal grunts and hungry gestures –
so much a noise that might come from my own mouth,

I can't tell us apart. When I do, daughter, I'll admit, I'm lost,
my new body wandering the forest,
dropping trails of bright stones
till I find you again, a new friend in an old place.

And for how many nights will it be this way,
this slow process of making and undoing,
the soft osmosis of your fragile body? My willing you not
to slip away, turning my own blue veins

to ice? I watch sand gather at your eyes' corners,
shadows making your face from nothing,
those eyes, which might turn any colour,
flickering, half-open, in the pages of your sleep.

I let them rise inside me, birds cased in glass.
And all the while snow falls, depositing on lawns and roofs
its subtle metamorphic chemistry.
Days drift to your smiles.

And I watch the pink coil of your ear,
the snub nose of beginnings;
count to myself in this lonely country
the hoots of an owl, a line of trees,

the bright rings of your growth.

Acknowledgements

Thanks to Liverpool Hope University College and the Arts and Humanities Research Board who gave me financial support and teaching relief in order to write this book. The quote that begins 'A Sky Canoe' is from Coleridge's 'Dejection Ode'; the poem Fay finds in Mara's notebook in 'Square One' is from Christina Rossetti's poem, 'A Chilly Night'. 'Clone' is a clone of Paul Muldoon's poem, 'As', published in *Moy Sand and Gravel* (Faber, 2003). Thanks to the editors of *Poetry Review* where 'Quiver' first appeared.